UNDERSEA UNIVERSITY™

THE Ocean Explorer's HANDBOOK

by
Fiona Bayrock

with **Mary Cerullo**
Consultant

SCHOLASTIC INC.

New York Toronto London Auckland Sydney
Mexico City New Delhi Hong Kong Buenos Aires

Fiona Bayrock
WRITER

Fiona writes about science from her home near the Pacific Ocean. Since she was a kid, she has loved beachcombing, tide pool hopping, and the feeling of waves burying her feet in the sand.

Mary Cerullo
CONSULTANT

Mary has been teaching and writing about the ocean for thirty years. She lives in Maine and works as the associate director of Friends of Casco Bay, an organization that protects and studies the bay.

ISBN: 0-439-71184-3
Copyright © 2005 by Scholastic Inc.

Designer: Mark Neely
Illustrators: Yancey C. Labat, Ed Shems, Zeke Smith, Shawn Gould

Photos:
Front cover: James Watt/Visuals Unlimited. Back cover: Wayne Levin/Taxi/Getty Images.
Page 2: (shell and starfish) Photodisc/Getty Images. Pages 4–5: (background) Philippe Poulet/Mission/Getty Images; (triops) Claude Van Lingen.
Page 8: (octopus) Jeffrey L. Rotman/Corbis; (probe) OAR/National Undersea Research Program/Harbor Branch Oceanographic Inst.
Page 9: (archaeologist) Alexis Rosenfeld/Photo Researchers; (ocean floor) W. Haxby/Lamont-Doherty Earth Observatory/Photo Researchers;
(oil spill) NOAA Restoration Center, SE region. Pages 10–11 and 46–47: (Earth) NASA/R. Stöckli/Robert Simmon/GSFC/MODIS.
Page 12: (Earth) NASA; (asteroids) The Image Bank/Getty Images. Page 15: Sinclair Stammers/Photo Researchers. Page 16: (top) Courtesy of Triops, Inc.;
(middle) Scott T. Smith/Corbis; (bottom) Robin Williams/Ecoscene/Corbis. Page 17: (top) Claude Van Lingen; (bottom) D. Bringard/Peter Arnold.
Page 23: (background) Alexis Rosenfeld/Photo Researchers; (upper left) Jim Zuckerman; (upper right) Dan Bigelow/The Image Bank/Getty Images;
(bottom left) David Trood Pictures/The Image Bank/Getty Images; (bottom right) Victoria Pearson/Stone/Getty Images.
Page 24: G. Brad Lewis/Photo Researchers. Page 25: Marli Miller/Visuals Unlimited. Page 28: Courtesy of Curt Ebbesmeyer.
Page 31: (hurricane) NASA/GSFC. Page 43: (*Titanic*) SPL/Photo Researchers; (Argo) Ralph White/Corbis;
(*Titanic* bow) National Oceanic and Atmospheric Administration/Department of Commerce.
Page 46: (Mauna Kea) Robin Scagell/Photo Researchers; (Weddell Sea) British Antarctic Survey/Photo Researchers.
Page 47: (Barrier Reef) David Fleetham/Visuals Unlimited. Page 48: Jeff Divine/Getty Images.

12 11 10 9 8 7   7 8 9/0

Printed in the U.S.A.
First Scholastic printing, January 2005
The publisher has made every effort to ensure that the activities in this book are safe when done as instructed.
Adults should provide guidance and supervision whenever the activity requires.

Table of Contents

page 18

page 41

page 38

Welcome to Undersea

Ahoy there, ocean explorer! Are you ready for an amazing undersea adventure? Ready to get to know creatures unlike any you'll find on land? Then you've joined the right club! Because here at Undersea University, you'll dive deep and discover a whole new world underwater! Be on the lookout for...

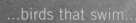
...whales that sing...

...birds that swim...

...fish that glow in the dark...

...sharks that smell blood from miles away...

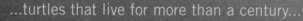
...turtles that live for more than a century...

...fish that tie themselves in knots...

...giant squid with eyes the size of volleyballs...

...fish that look like rocks...

...and lots of other wonders as you tour the seas. If you thought you'd have to travel to another planet to explore a different world, think again—the oceans of your own planet are right here and waiting for you to dive in!

University!

What'll I Do at Undersea U?

As a member of the Undersea U crew, you'll take a grand tour of Earth's oceans. You'll encounter everything from sea horses and stingrays to shipwrecks and pirates! By the time your deep-sea journey is through, you'll be an expert ocean explorer with an official *Deep*-loma to show for it!

What's This Book All About?

This is your handbook, the first book in the Undersea University series. It's the starting place for all your ocean adventures! As you swim through the pages of your handbook, you'll find:

Sea Quests and Mini-Quests

Sea Quests are fun activities that'll help make you a real seaworthy explorer. You'll grow your own prehistoric underwater pets called triops, create a mini-submarine model, make a map of an ocean floor, create your own rain—and much more!

triops

Mini-Quests are also floating through these pages for you to try and *sea*! These quick splashes will keep you in the flow and in the know.

Here's what else you'll find in your handbook:

"Whale of a Tale" Stories

These tales are true stories of ocean adventures, discoveries, disasters, and mysteries. When you read these sea tales, you'll splash beneath the surface of undersea history.

"Words from the Water Wise" Interviews

Here's where you'll meet ocean experts and explorers. These water-wise whizzes will give you the inside scoop on what it means to follow your questions and bring the answers to the surface.

Info Bubbles

As you swim through your handbook, be sure to stop at the bubbles you find along the way. These Info Bubbles will reveal cool undersea facts to add to your pool of ocean smarts.

The Undersea University Website

Guess what, ocean explorer? Undersea U has a website! So if you like to surf—*web* surf, that is—you're in luck. Visit the site at **www.scholastic.com/undersea**, and you'll discover great undersea challenges and games. Just make sure to bring along your secret password (below), because only Undersea U ocean explorers can enter the site!

P.S. With each new book, you'll get a new password to access more fun on the Undersea U website. You'll find each password surfing a wave just like this one in every Undersea U book!

WEB-SURFING PASSWORD

GETWET

What's in Your Sea Chest?

Every month you'll receive an Undersea Kit filled with cool stuff to help you get the most from your undersea adventures. Here's what's in your kit this month:

Grow-Your-Own Triops Kit
You've got all the supplies you need to hatch and raise your very own prehistoric pets—creatures called triops! Splash over to page 18 to get started!

Tank for Your Triops

Magnifier
With this magnifier, you'll be able to get a close-up look at your baby triops as they grow!

Mini-Sub Kit
Send this sub down to the depths, then make it rise again—with just a squeeze of your hand. Float on over to page 41 to *sink* into this activity!

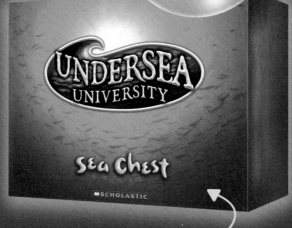

Gulp! Card Game
Get to know "who eats who" under the sea—from big predators to tiny creatures too small to see. Swim to page 38 to start gulping!

Stay Seaworthy!

Some Sea Quests will require some help from a "*sea*-nior" (adult) adviser. Just check the "Your Crew" section in the Sea Quest instructions to see when this is the case. Adults help keep Sea Quests safe, mate!

Undersea University Sea Chest
Your Sea Chest is a great place to store the undersea gear you'll be getting throughout your Undersea U adventures. Keep it handy so you'll be ready for whatever swims your way!

Ocean Science Rocks!

How many kinds of scientists does it take to study something as big as an ocean? Lots! Fortunately, there's one big word that covers all the ocean sciences: *oceanography*. Below you can read about just some of the sciences that oceanography includes. By the time you're an Undersea U grad, you'll be an expert in *all* of these areas!

INFO BUBBLE

"Marine" is another word for "ocean."

Put "marine" in front of any science and it instantly becomes an ocean science, as you can see below.

OCEAN

Marine Biology
Biology is the study of life, so marine biology is the study of ocean life. Marine biologists want to know about anything that lives in the ocean or really close to it. This includes plants and animals buried in the seafloor, creatures crawling on the beach, or anything that swims in the sea. As you can probably guess, the field of marine biology is gigantic! Want to know more? Check out pages 32-37.

Ocean Exploration
Believe it or not, scientists know more about the surface of the Moon than they do about the bottom of the ocean! But thanks to great new probes and deep-sea vehicles, every year ocean explorers see more of the ocean than ever before. Turn to page 40 to start exploring the undersea frontier!

This undersea vehicle carries scientists down to the darkest depths, where they can observe and collect samples.

Marine Archaeology Imagine exploring a shipwreck and finding treasures that haven't been touched for hundreds of years—that's the job of a marine archaeologist! The treasures they find give them clues to the lives of the people that the ships once carried. Dive over to page 43 to read about the hunt for the *Titanic*!

OGRAPHY

Marine Geology Imagine if you could empty the ocean, just for a minute. You'd see volcanoes and cliffs, wide flowing plains, mountains taller than Mount Everest, and valleys deeper than the Grand Canyon. It's hard to imagine that such spectacular sights exist underwater, but they do!

Marine geologists are interested in these undersea structures and the way they're changed by earthquakes, volcanoes, landslides, and more. But how do marine geologists find out what the ocean floor looks like? Turn to page 44 to see for yourself!

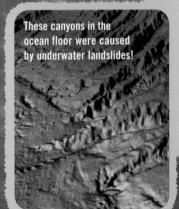

These canyons in the ocean floor were caused by underwater landslides!

An oil spill on a beach in Florida

Marine Ecology When a big ship spills oil into the ocean, the results are *not* pretty (as you can see on the right). How can we clean up messes like this? And how can we protect our oceans from other kinds of pollution? These are exactly the kinds of questions that marine ecologists work on. If you want to know how we can keep our oceans healthy far into the future, then stay tuned, ocean explorer—Undersea U will make sure you're in the know!

Water, Water,
— Everywhere!

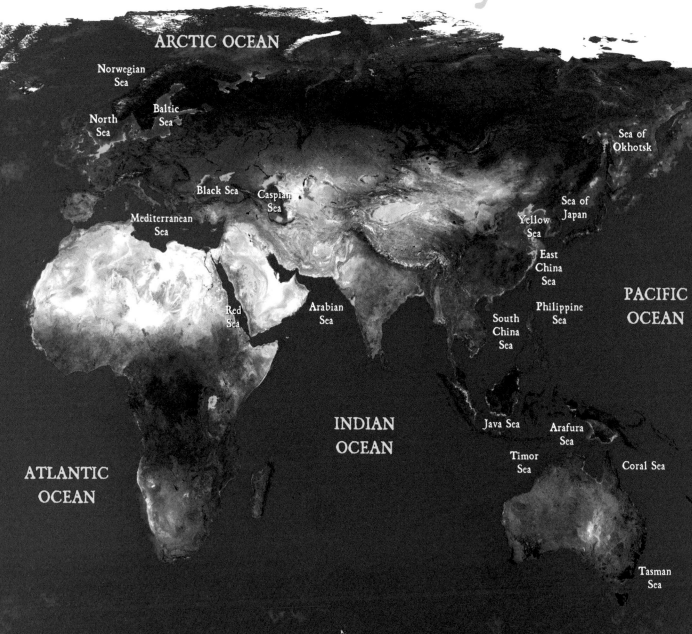

ARCTIC OCEAN

Norwegian
Sea

North
Sea

Baltic
Sea

Sea of
Okhotsk

Be
S

Black Sea

Caspian
Sea

Sea of
Japan

Mediterranean
Sea

Yellow
Sea

East
China
Sea

PACIFIC
OCEAN

Red
Sea

Arabian
Sea

Philippine
Sea

South
China
Sea

INDIAN
OCEAN

Java Sea

Arafura
Sea

Timor
Sea

Coral Sea

ATLANTIC
OCEAN

Tasman
Sea

SOUTHERN OCEAN

How many oceans does Earth have—five or one? If you said *five*, you're right, and if you said *one*, you're *also* right! The Earth has five oceans—Pacific, Atlantic, Indian, Arctic, and Southern—and they all connect together, so you could say we have one big ocean! Take a look at the map below, and you'll see how each ocean flows into the next.

Chukchi Sea

ATLANTIC OCEAN

Sargasso Sea

Caribbean Sea

Amundsen Sea

Weddell Sea

Ocean? Sea? What's the Difference?

Good question! Seas are smaller areas set off from the rest of an ocean—usually, they're partly surrounded by land. Take a look at the seas on this map and you'll *sea*!

mini Quest

Water, Water, Everywhere!

Check out just how much water there is on this blue planet of ours!

1. Grab a globe, close your eyes, and give the globe a good spin.

2. As the globe is whirling around, place your finger on it until it stops. Is your finger touching land or water? (You'll need to open your eyes to check!)

3. Spin the globe ten times and keep track of where your finger lands. How many times did you hit water?

You should have found that your finger hit water about seven out of ten times, or 70 percent of the time. That's because about 70 percent of the planet is covered in water! So if you like to swim, you're in luck—there are more places to swim on this planet than there are to walk!

The Early Oceans

The Blue Planet

From space, Earth looks blue, thanks to water covering almost three-quarters of its surface. As you'll soon discover, that's what makes Earth such a good place to live.

Did the Earth Always Have Oceans?

Nope! When the Earth first formed billions of years ago, it was a raging hot ball of melted rock—way too hot for oceans! But then, as the Earth slowly cooled, temperatures became just right for liquid water to collect on the surface.

Where Did All That Water Come From?

Scientists have lots of ideas, but no one knows for sure. Many think the water came from space—riding aboard icy asteroids that crashed onto the surface of young Planet Earth!

Earth was hit by lots of asteroids in its early years, so it's possible that these huge, icy rocks brought the water that now fills our oceans.

With all this water, it seems like our planet should be called Planet Ocean, not Planet Earth!

How Did the Oceans Take Shape?

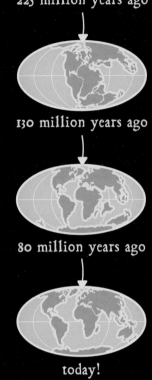

Panthalassa   Pangaea
225 million years ago

130 million years ago

80 million years ago

today!

Earth's oceans didn't always look like they do today. Read on to find out how they formed!

Sea Back in Time!

Hundreds of millions of years ago, Earth had one big continent called Pangaea (pan-JEE-uh), and one huge ocean called Panthalassa.

Then, slowly, over millions of years, Pangaea split apart, forming the continents and oceans you know today. And guess what—the continents are *still* moving!

Whoa! The Continents Are MOVING?

That's right. But don't worry—no need to hang on tight. The distance the continents move each year is so small, it's measured in centimeters.

And *why* do the continents move? Good question! It's because the Earth's hard outer layer, called the *crust*, is broken up into pieces. These pieces, called *plates*, float on top of a bed of hot melted rock. As the plates slowly drift toward each other or slide apart, the Earth's continents and oceans take on whole new shapes, as you can see above!

Now that you've read about how the oceans formed, turn the page to get to know H₂O!

Pass the Plates, Please!

Head over to the Undersea U website (**www.scholastic.com/undersea**) and try your hand at moving continents around! Remember to bring your password, which you'll find riding the wave on page 6.

The Wonders of Water

You know the *oceans* are full of water, but how much of *your* body is made up of water, ocean explorer? Would you believe 50 to 70 percent? That means more than half of you is nothing but good old H_2O!

It should come as no surprise that you need water to survive. If you were stuck somewhere without food, you could live for six weeks or more, but if you were stuck without water, you'd be lucky to live a week!

In fact, water is essential to all life as we know it—it's part of every living thing on the planet! Why does water have what it takes to support life? Read on to find out!

What's So Special About Water?

● **Water changes temperature VERY slowly!** On a hot day at the beach, the ocean water can still be cool and refreshing, right? That's because it takes a lot more heat to warm up water than it does to warm up land.

Likewise, water cools down much more slowly than land does. As water cools, it releases lots of heat, warming the air above it. Nights on Earth would be a lot colder than they are now if it weren't for water holding onto the heat of the day, keeping our air warm.

So, thanks to water keeping temperatures steady, life under the sea *and* on land can count on a comfortable, stable place to live.

INFO BUBBLE

Water is the only substance we can find naturally on Earth as a solid, liquid, and gas.

● **Water is a great dissolver!** If you stir sugar into water, it dissolves, right? Well, water can dissolve oxygen and other gases, too. This is great news for sea creatures, because that dissolved oxygen is what they breathe!

You can see these gases yourself if you grab an ice cube and look at it through your magnifier. You'll see little white specks or streaks—these are bubbles of gas that were dissolved in the water when it was still liquid. When the water froze solid, the gas came out of the water solution.

● **Ice floats!** When other substances go from a liquid to a solid (like metals, for example), they shrink as their molecules squeeze together into a solid form. Not water! Water *expands* when it freezes. Why? Because when water changes to ice, the molecules bond in a way that leaves tiny spaces between them. This makes ice lighter than water, so ice floats. Ocean *surfaces* may freeze solid, but the water underneath stays liquid, making it a great home for sea creatures.

Imagine if ice sank instead. The Sun's heat couldn't reach the ice on the ocean bottom to melt it, so it would stay frozen. As more water froze and sank, the oceans around the North and South Poles would eventually become permanent blocks of ice. That's some ice rink— but not a good place for life!

INFO BUBBLE

What Is Water?

Water, like everything else in the universe, is made up of atoms. To make water, two hydrogen atoms and one oxygen atom have to join together to form one water *molecule*. A-ha! That's where the scientific name "H_2O" comes from!

oxygen →

hydrogen →   hydrogen ←

H_2O

Get a Life!

Since water is so important to life, most scientists agree that life on Earth probably began in the ocean.

The oldest rock fossils, 3,600 million years old, show tiny one-celled organisms that look like blue-green algae. Nowadays, microscopic floating plants like these are still around— we call them *phytoplankton* (flip to page 33 to get the scoop on these tiny organisms). Like the plants you see on land, these tiny aquatic plants give off oxygen as they use energy from the Sun to make food (a process called *photosynthesis*).

Thanks to ancient algae, the atmosphere of young planet Earth became rich with oxygen. That made conditions just right for lots of oxygen-loving creatures (like you!) to evolve on Earth.

blue-green algae

In the billions of years since the first life appeared in the oceans, all sorts of underwater creatures have lived on our planet. You're about to meet one that's been around for 240 million years—and soon to be swimming in your very own tank!

Introducing...

Triops:
Your Pets
from the Dinosaur Days!

Move over, goldfish! Triops are no ordinary underwater pet. They were around when the first dinosaurs roamed the Earth, and they're *still* here, exactly as they were way back then. Talk about standing the test of time!

What Are Triops?

Triops are *crustaceans*—animals with hard outer shells, like horseshoe crabs, lobsters, and shrimp. Triops hatch from tiny eggs and grow very quickly to their adult size, which is about 2 inches (5 cm) long. They have a short life span—usually a few weeks (ninety days is a ripe old age for triops!). Triops are great pets to watch as they grow, because they can double in size daily!

Where Do Triops Live?

Triops live in freshwater ponds all over the world (though your triops eggs came from a special aquatic farm). Triops are not ocean creatures— they don't live in salt water—but they're similar to some marine animals you'll meet later on at Undersea U (like shrimp and other crustaceans).

Triops live in many different parts of the world because back when they first appeared, Earth had just one big continent, Pangaea (back up to page 13 if this is news to you!). When Pangaea split up, triops ended up on many continents around the world.

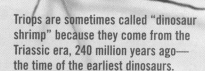

Triops are sometimes called "dinosaur shrimp" because they come from the Triassic era, 240 million years ago— the time of the earliest dinosaurs.

Some people think triops look like horseshoe crabs. Do you see any similarity? Like triops, horseshoe crabs have been around for hundreds of millions of years.

The fairy shrimp is another crustacean that looks a lot like your triops.

Three Eyes!
Triops got their name because they have three eyes ("tri" means "three" and "ops" means "eyes"). Once your triops have grown big enough, see if you can spot all three eyes with your magnifier (the third one in the middle is the smallest and the toughest to see).

third eye

Abdomen

Lots o' Legs
Triops have between thirty-five and seventy-one pairs of legs. They use their legs to swim, to burrow through sand in search of food, to bring food to their mouths, and to breathe! That's right, triops breathe through their legs! In dirty water, you'll see your triops swim upside down and sweep the surface for air. (This is a good sign that you should clean your tank water!)

Antennae

Hard Outer Shell
The hard outer shell is called the "exoskeleton" (which means "outside skeleton"). As triops grow, they shed their exoskeletons and grow new, bigger ones. Look for their old exoskeletons at the bottom of your tank!

How Did Triops Outlive the Dinosaurs?

Triops have stood the test of time for one very good reason—their eggs are built to last! Triops live in ponds that dry up during times of the year when there's no rainfall. Adult triops die when the water dries up, but their eggs develop thick shells and wait till the water comes back—as long as fifteen years! These hardy eggs allowed the triops species to survive long periods of drought while other animals died out.

Dinosaurs from Triassic times like this one couldn't last through the ages—but triops managed to survive!

One...Two... Triops!

Grab your triops kit, ocean explorer, because it's time to hatch your prehistoric pets! Your almost-invisible eggs are about to turn into swimming, flipping, zooming creatures—just like the ones that existed way back when dinosaurs roamed the Earth! (Flip back a page if you haven't already traveled back to early triops times!)

Here's what's in your triops kit:

Triops Eggs
These teeny-tiny specks will hatch once they're placed in water.

Hatching Nutrients
Put these in the water to help your triops grow.

Triops Food
The green pellets are made of algae, and the brown ones are made of animal protein.

Thermometer
Triops need to live in warm water—use this to keep tabs on water temps! The green bar marks the temperature. If you see tan and blue bars, the temperature is between those bars.

Sand
When your triops grow up, you can add sand to the tank and watch them play!

Pipette
Use this like a vacuum to keep your tank clean.

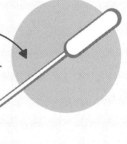

What You Need
- Triops kit *
- Clear plastic disposable cup
- 1 gallon of spring water (room temperature)
- Toothpick
- Desk lamp
- Triops tank *
- Magnifier *
- Plain paper
- Spoon
- Aluminum foil

* In your Sea Chest
UNDERSEA UNIVERSITY

Your crew
- An adult adviser to help you raise your triops

What You Do
Part 1: Egg-cellent Start!

Day 1:

1. Find a clear plastic disposable cup and rinse it out. Don't use soap—it may be harmful to your triops.

2. Stick the thermometer from your triops kit to the outside of the cup.

3. Fill the cup with 2 inches (5 cm) of spring water.

4. Add about one-fourth of the container of hatching nutrients to the water, using a toothpick to push the nutrients in.

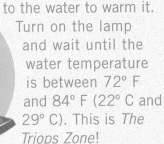

5. Set the cup under the lamp, making sure that the light is close enough to the water to warm it. Turn on the lamp and wait until the water temperature is between 72° F and 84° F (22° C and 29° C). This is *The Triops Zone*!

6. **Warning:** Triops eggs are tiny and will blow away. So do this next step away from drafts and don't breathe on the eggs. Once the water temperature is in *The Triops Zone*, carefully open the egg container over the cup (so if any eggs fall out, they'll fall into the cup).

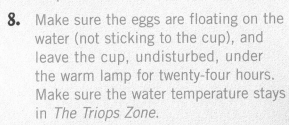

7. Use a toothpick to nudge ten to fifteen triops eggs into the cup. Not all the eggs! Why? Because if you save some eggs, you can hatch more triops later!

8. Make sure the eggs are floating on the water (not sticking to the cup), and leave the cup, undisturbed, under the warm lamp for twenty-four hours. Make sure the water temperature stays in *The Triops Zone*.

9. In a few days, your hatched triops are going to be ready to move out of the cup and into your tank. So, get that tank ready for them! Start by rinsing it out (no soap here, either!).

10. Fill the tank with spring water (up to about 1 inch [2.5 cm] from the top) and add a tiny pinch of hatching nutrients. Place the tank under the lamp beside the cup. That way, the tank water will be just like the water in the cup when your triops are ready to move!

The Triops Zone

Triops Zone=72° F to 84° F (22° C to 29° C). For happy, healthy triops, keep your triops water temperature in *The Triops Zone*, using the lamp for warmth. Triops will grow faster in warm water, but if the temperature drops below

°F	°C
84	29
82	28
80	27
78	26
76	24
74	23
72	22

72° F (22° C), your eggs may not hatch, or your triops may die. In warm weather, you may not need the lamp to keep the water warm, but make sure your triops get about twelve hours of light a day.

Days 2 and 3: Grab your magnifier and check out those baby triops! How many hatched? You should expect between one and three triops. Are they growing quickly?

Day 4: Today is feeding day! Woo-hoo!

I. To feed your triops, fold a piece of paper in half and put one green and one brown food pellet inside the folded paper.

2. Crush the pellets into powder with a spoon.

What Happened to My Missing Triops?

There's something you should know about triops—they're *cannibalistic*. That means they eat each other! The bigger and stronger triops will eat the small, weak, or sick ones. If you notice one of your triops is missing, it was probably a snack for its neighbor!

If you want to prevent your triops from snacking on each other, keep the bigger ones in separate tanks. Any clean plastic container can work as a tank (or you can buy a fancy one from a pet store). Just make sure to warm up the water in your new tank before dropping in your triops.

3. Holding the two edges of the folded paper, let the food fall into the fold. Then pour about a quarter of the food into the cup and save the rest in the folded paper for Day 6. Watch your hungry triops chow down!

Day 5: Don't feed your triops today. They don't have a big enough appetite yet! Just check 'em out with your magnifier. How much have they grown since yesterday?

Day 6: Feed your triops a little more—about half a green pellet and half a brown pellet. (Your saved food from Day 4 should do the trick!)

Day 7: If your triops have eaten all the food you gave them yesterday, make a fresh crushed pellet mix and feed them the same amount again.

Part 2: Growing Up!

Day 8:

I. Peel the thermometer from the cup and stick it to the outside of the tank to see if the tank temperature is in *The Triops Zone*. If the temperature's all right, slowly pour the baby triops, water and all, from cup to tank. Add more spring water, if necessary, to bring the water level about ½ inch (1 cm) from the top.

2. Place a piece of foil over one-third of the tank to give your triops a shady rest area.

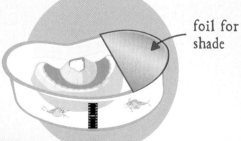

foil for shade

Day 9: Add one crushed food pellet per triops. If they eat everything within a few hours, give them more. Alternate green and brown pellets.

Day 10: Remove leftover hatching nutrients by sucking them up with the pipette. Feed your triops as you did on Day 9.

Day 11 and beyond: Feed your triops on a regular schedule—one pellet per triops in the morning and one again at night is about right. If your triops eat all this food in one day, you can feed them a little more. If you want your triops to grow larger, you can even try feeding them very small bits of peeled carrot or shrimp twice a week.

To make sure your triops stay healthy, you'll also need to keep the tank clean and change the water every week. Check out the box below to learn how!

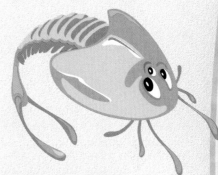

How Do I Keep My Tank Clean?

Out with the Fuzzies!
When uneaten food, waste, and old triops shells (exoskeletons) collect at the bottom of the tank, the water can start looking a little fuzzy! To clear things up, just use your pipette to suck the "fuzzies" away! Here's how:

First, squirt the pipette underwater to gather the "fuzzies" into one spot in the tank. Then slowly "vacuum" them up and release the dirty pipette water into the toilet. Vacuuming the fuzzies every few days will help keep the water clean and clear.

Freshen Up!
Change the tank water every week, or more often if it gets green or dirty. Before adding fresh spring water, keep the water under the lamp next to the tank for a day so it's the same temperature as the tank water. Then, follow these steps:

1. Fill a clean plastic cup with warm spring water.
2. Use a clean plastic spoon to move your triops into the cup.
3. Carefully pour the dirty tank water into the toilet.
4. Refill the tank with warm spring water, and pour your triops back in!

Part 3: Triops Tricks

When your triops are all grown up, try some triops tricks:

▶ **Fun with Sand!**
Rinse out the sand by swishing it around with water in a disposable cup. Then wait for the sand to settle before pouring the water (not the sand) into the toilet. Let the sand dry out overnight and then pour it onto the raised part of your tank. Your triops will move the sand around and play in it, using their legs to sift through the grains.

▶ **Play *Food*ball!** Feed your triops whole pellets instead of crushed ones. They'll often lie on their backs and hang onto the pellets like they're playing ball!

▶ **Acrobat Swimmers!** Your triops won't need any help with this trick. Triops like to be on the move! Watch them flip and zoom around the tank!

How Long Will My Triops Live?

Like other pets, triops need three things: food, oxygen, and a good place to live. So, if you feed them well, keep the water clean, and make sure their tank temperature is in *The Triops Zone*, your triops will live long lives—for triops, that is! Even in the best conditions, triops live only twenty to ninety days. And triops grow at different rates, too. If you keep the food coming and the water temperature at the top end of *The Triops Zone*, your triops will grow up faster.

Start Fresh!

When your triops die, empty the tank into the toilet, then thoroughly rinse out the tank. Wipe off all algae and dry off the tank with a paper towel. Then you can start over! You have enough food, eggs, and hatching nutrients to do three hatchings. If you run out of food, you can substitute fish pellet food (which you can find at pet stores), and give your triops occasional snacks of shrimp and peeled carrot. You can also buy more sand at a pet store.

PART 2

Ocean Basics

Now that you're back from your trip through Earth's early oceans, it's time to get to know the oceans today, and get a handle on the basics that every ocean explorer needs to know! Let's start by answering one big question…

Why Is the Ocean Blue?

Wait a second—*is* the ocean really blue? Have you ever seen the ocean looking green? Or turquoise? Or gray? In fact, the ocean can be any of these colors!

Clear ocean water often looks blue because of the way water reflects sunlight. Shallow water usually looks bright turquoise, and deeper water is a deeper blue.

There's also *another* reason for blue water: The ocean looks blue because it mirrors the blue sky. On a cloudy day when the sky is gray, you'll find the ocean looking grayer.

But the color of the ocean isn't limited to shades of blue and gray! It can look green, brown, or even orange or red—these colors show up when dirt or tiny animals called plankton are floating in the water.

Pass the Salt!

Ocean water sure is salty—*bleh*! Don't drink it! It contains about a cup of salt per gallon! Where does all that salt come from? Well, it starts off in soil and rocks, and then it gets rinsed into streams and rivers by rainwater. These rivers eventually carry the salt into the ocean. When ocean water evaporates under the Sun's heat, the salt stays behind—making the water salty!

Grab your surfboard, ocean explorer! Surfing through the next few pages will give you a complete look at the many ways the ocean is in motion!

Surf's Up!

What's the first ocean motion that comes to mind? If you said "waves," you're not alone! But waves aren't *only* found in the ocean—you can also find waves in lakes, pools, bathtubs, or even in puddles!

How Are Waves Made?

WIND + WATER = WAVES. That's it, pure and simple. Anytime you have wind and water together, you have waves. You can make waves yourself just by blowing on a bowl of soup!

Ocean waves usually start with a gentle breeze blowing on the surface to make ripples. As the wind blows longer and stronger, the ripples grow into waves of energy that travel across the water.

Why Do Waves Crash?

Closer to shore, the water becomes shallower until the bottom of each wave meets the seafloor. This slows the bottom of the wave, but not the top. The wave basically trips over itself and the top part crashes onto the shore. There you have it—"breaking" waves.

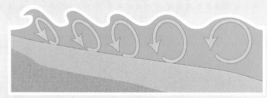

When the bottom of the wave meets the seafloor, the wave "trips" and crashes onto the shore.

The Ins and Outs of Tides

Have you ever spent hours building a sand castle at the beach, only to have waves creep up and wash it away?

In some way or another, if you've been to the beach, you've seen the effects of the *tides*. Tides go in and out on seacoasts all over the world once or twice a day (depending on where you are). High tides bring water high up on the beach, carrying all sorts of undersea stuff to shore (like seashells, driftwood, and animals that come along for the ride). Then low tides pull the water away.

high tide

low tide

What Causes Tides?

Tides happen when the pull of gravity from the Moon causes the Earth's water to bulge out. As the Earth turns, the bulging areas move across the ocean (because they're always aligned with the Moon), and this high water causes high tides. In parts of the world where the water *isn't* bulging, it's low tide.

If you want to see how this works, try the Mini-Quest below!

Fit to Be Tide

Here's a quick way to see how the Moon's gravity causes high and low tides!

mini Quest

1. Fill a shallow, clear, rectangular baking dish half full of water.

2. Float a piece of cardboard in the water. It should be about the length of the dish (try cutting it out of a cereal box).

3. Gently lift up one end of the baking dish and rest it on a pen or pencil.

4. Look at your baking dish from the side and notice how deep the water is at each end. Where is the water "bulging" away from the cardboard?

Here's what's going on in your baking dish: When you tilt the dish, gravity pulls the water down to the low end. This makes the water bulge away from the cardboard to create a high tide. In the same way, the Moon's gravity creates high tides by pulling water away from Earth. The other end of your dish, where the water beneath the cardboard is shallower, represents a low tide.

gravity causes a bulge

Current Events!

Would you believe there are *rivers* flowing through the ocean? There sure are—and they're called *currents*. Read on to get the drift!

Huh? Rivers in the Ocean?

That's right. Just like we have rivers that carry water across land, currents carry water through the oceans. Thanks to currents, the same water will eventually travel through all five oceans!

There are two different kinds of currents—*surface* currents and *deepwater* currents. Surface currents are usually created by wind blowing on the water. Deepwater currents are powered by a very different process—you'll find out all about them on page 29!

The map below shows you the paths of surface currents around the world. Check 'em out, and then flow over to the next page to read about the adventures of current-riding sneakers, rubber duckies, and more!

Way to Flow!
The locations of islands and continents help shape the paths of surface currents.

Round and Round We Go!

Because the Earth spins, surface currents traveling straight south or north don't actually travel straight. Instead they curve—to the left in the Southern Hemisphere, and to the right in the Northern Hemisphere. This is called the Coriolis effect, named after Gustave-Gaspard Coriolis, the scientist who discovered it in 1835.

These curving currents eventually brush up against land and create circular patterns called *gyres*, which you see here.

Full Stream Ahead!

The Gulf Stream is a super-strong surface current in the Atlantic Ocean. It's huge! It carries more water than all of the rivers in the world combined, bringing warm water from the south up the coast of North America and across to Europe.

The Gulf Stream *also* brings warm weather with it, making the climate in northern Europe much warmer than it would be otherwise.

Riding the Currents

Have you ever picked up something washed up on the beach and wondered how it got there? Things that float around the ocean, riding the surface currents, are called *flotsam*. Check out the stories of some wacky world-traveling flotsam below!

Message in a Bottle

A wealthy woman named Daisy Singer Alexander threw a bottle into the Thames River in England in 1937. The message inside said whoever found the bottle would get half of her money. The bottle cruised the currents for twelve years until a man named Jack Wurm found it on a California beach. When he pulled out the note, he was amazed to find out that he would inherit six million dollars!

Just Ducky!

In 1992, about 29,000 rubber duckies and other bath toys fell overboard traveling from China to Seattle, Washington. Observing and tracking how the toys floated around the planet has helped oceanographers learn more about how currents work.

Lego to the Rescue!

Almost five million Lego pieces (including thousands of plastic flippers and tiny life rafts!) fell off a ship near England in 1997. Some pieces are expected to ride the currents to beaches all the way over on the west coast of the United States!

Sneaking Around the Planet

In May 1990, shipping containers fell off a cargo ship, spilling 80,000 sneakers into the Pacific Ocean. Surface currents carried some of the shoes to beaches in Oregon, Washington, and British Columbia, and others drifted as far as Hawaii, the Philippines, and Japan. Some shoes stayed afloat for ten years!

OCEANOGRAPHER
Dr. Curt Ebbesmeyer

Curt Ebbesmeyer holding a device that records the weather over the ocean

Give a big *wave* to **Dr. Curt Ebbesmeyer**, an oceanographer who's more like an ocean detective! He uses what he knows about ocean currents to solve the mysteries behind flotsam that washes up on the beach (check out page 27 for some weird examples!).

When Dr. Ebbesmeyer first became an oceanographer in the 1970s, he tracked serious things like oil spills and sewage. Then, in 1991, his mom read about lots of sneakers washing ashore and asked him to find out where they came from. Ever since, Dr. Ebbesmeyer has been tracing the histories of flotsam like rubber ducks, computers, Legos, basketballs, hockey gloves—you name it!

Question: How did you become interested in oceanography?

Answer: As a kid, I saw a hydrographic chart (a chart of how the ocean floor looks without water) and thought, "Wow, that's really cool!" Later, I started scuba diving, and I really loved being in the ocean.

Q: Why are you interested in ocean currents?

A: When something washes up, I want to know: What's the real story behind it? Where did it come from? How long did it take to reach the shore?

Q: How does flotsam help you track currents?

A: Every year, thousands of shipping containers fall overboard, so you begin to get a glimpse of the enormous potential of following all this stuff. Each of the Nike shoes that spilled in 1990 (see page 27) had a serial number, so I have the possibility of finding out where 80,000 things went from one point in the ocean!

Q: How do you predict where flotsam will land?

A: I use a computer model of the currents and winds across the North Pacific Ocean, called OSCURS (which stands for **O**cean **S**urface **CUR**rent **S**imulation), designed by oceanographer Jim Ingraham. I can put an object into the North Pacific and OSCURS will move it along by the currents and winds day by day. I can also tell it where an object started and ended anywhere in the North Pacific, and the model tells me how it got there.

Q: So things we find on the beach can be the start of serious science?

A: You bet! It gets us to a better understanding of the ocean. The beach is mostly about curiosity. When you go to the beach, have fun. Look for things that float. Check bottles for messages. Be curious. It amazes me when people go to the beach just to get a tan—that's like going to Disneyland and staying in the parking lot!

Go Deep!

Now that you're up to speed on *surface* currents, it's time to dive deeper and discover another kind of current—*deepwater* currents.

Sailors first realized that these deep currents existed centuries ago, when they dropped buckets deep into the ocean and hauled up icy cold water. Where did this water come from? The sailors *thought* it came from the North or South Pole, but they couldn't figure out why cold water would flow away from the poles. Get ready to find out why by making your own deepwater current!

What You Need

- Tablespoon
- Water (warm and cold)
- Drinking glass
- Green food coloring (blue or red will also work just fine!)
- Shallow, clear, rectangular baking dish

What You Do

1. Add 3 tablespoons of cold water to the drinking glass.

2. Mix in 4 drops of food coloring.

3. Put the drinking glass in the refrigerator for twenty minutes.

4. Fill the baking dish a little more than three-quarters full with very warm tap water.

5. Slowly and gently, pour the green water from the glass into one end of the baking dish.

6. Get down and look at the side of the baking dish at eye level. Where did the green water go?

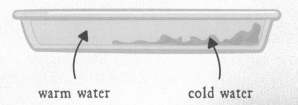

warm water   cold water

Sea the Point?

When you poured the cold green water into the baking dish, it sank. That's because cold water is *denser* (and therefore heavier) than warm water. Why? Because in cold water, the molecules squish together, which means there are *more* molecules in a drop of cold water than in a drop of warm water. That makes the cold water sink through the warm water!

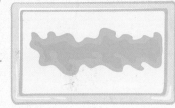

You should have *also* noticed that the cold water moved across the bottom of the baking dish. This happens because the sinking cold water shoves the warm water out of the way.

In the ocean, cold water at the North and South Poles sinks to the bottom of the ocean the same way that your green water did. The cold water creates deepwater currents as it moves under warm water and across the Earth!

Make Your Own Rain!

The ocean affects the weather in LOTS of ways, ocean explorer. Currents that carry warm water also bring along warm weather, heating up parts of the world that would otherwise be super chilly!

But there's another big way the ocean affects weather—and that's by giving us rain. Thanks to the ocean, we have an unlimited supply of wet weather! Want to see how rain forms? Try this Sea Quest to find out!

What You Do

I. Fill one cup three-quarters full with warm water.

2. Immediately turn the other cup upside down and place it on top of the first cup, rim to rim. Tape the cups together.

warm water

3. Place your cup tower on a warm, sunny windowsill or under a desk lamp.

4. Rest the bag of ice cubes on top of your cup tower.

5. Weather forecast: cloudy with a chance of rain. Watch your cup to see if the forecast is right!

bag of ice

What You Need

- Two clear plastic cups
- Warm water
- Tape
- Desk lamp or sunny window
- Sandwich bag of ice cubes

raindrops

Sea the Point?

As the Sun (or lamp) heated the water, some of it changed from liquid to water vapor (this is called *evaporation*). The vapor rose and hit the air cooled by the ice. The cold caused the vapor to change back into a liquid and form a cloud of tiny water droplets in the top cup (this is called *condensation*). All those tiny droplets kept bumping into each other, forming larger and larger drops until they were heavy enough to fall from the top of the cup—raindrops!

What happened in your cup tower is like what happens when rain forms on Earth, except on Earth there's plenty more water and bigger clouds, of course! The water in the bottom cup is like ocean water, evaporating as it gets heated up by the Sun, then condensing into clouds, and then falling as rain, only to evaporate all over again. The same water cycles through again and again as rain, snow, and hail, too.

Hurricane ALERT!

So, rainmaker, now that you know how the ocean puts the "wet" in wet weather—imagine what happens when things *really* heat up, and LOTS of water evaporates and whirls into a giant storm. That's a recipe for disaster!

Hey, Not So Fast!

A hurricane is a huge spiraling storm with super-fast winds. How fast? The strongest can reach speeds of more than 155 miles per hour (250 km/h)! That's faster than a speeding *train*!

Just How Dangerous Are Hurricanes, Anyway?

Imagine flying furniture...road signs blowing like leaves... roofs ripped off houses...and you can get a sense of the enormous destructive power of a hurricane. The worst hurricane on record, a storm that ripped through Galveston, Texas in 1900, wound up killing more than 6,000 people. Nowadays, weather experts can predict the paths of hurricanes—and warn people to get out of their way!

Galveston, Texas after a hurricane

Where Exactly Do Hurricanes Happen?

Hurricanes form over warm ocean waters and then move toward land. Islands in the Caribbean and states like Florida can get hit hard, because they're often right in the path of hurricanes when they reach shore. The good news? Hurricanes usually die down about a day after they reach land. But their destruction is never forgotten!

This hurricane whirled over the Atlantic in 1992. Storms like this in the Pacific Ocean are called "typhoons," while those in the Indian Ocean are called "cyclones."

PART 3: Livin' the Marine Life!

Did you know that 99 percent of all living space on Earth is in the ocean? Amazing, huh? In fact, the ocean is home-sweet-home to most of the world's animal species. Ocean explorers have found life on every level of the ocean, even way down deep, where there's little oxygen and no light.

Did Somebody Say LUNCH?

Animals rely on each other for food. Well, actually, they rely on each other to *be* food. Unless they're vegetarians that eat seaweed or other undersea plants, animals eat each other. The little creatures get eaten by bigger ones, and then predators (like sharks!) move in for their meals. This is often called a *food chain*, which you could imagine like this: ⟶

The Food Web

But really it's not as simple as a food *chain*. The same way you can't live by eating bananas alone, animals don't usually have just one item on their menus. Instead of a simple food chain, animals are part of a food *web*, like this:

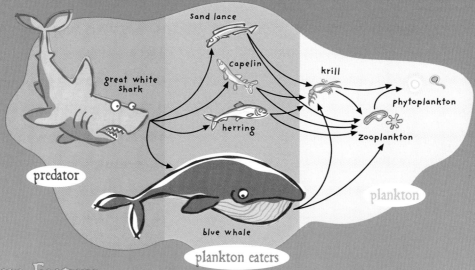

Creature Feature

On the next few pages, you'll make your way up the food web and meet the creatures featured on your Undersea U Gulp! cards. Then you'll be ready to gulp away when you get to page 38!

Welcome to the marine food web, ocean explorer! It all starts here, with super-tiny floating creatures we call...

Plankton!

What's the tiniest food in the ocean? You'll have to look really closely to find the itty-bitty plants and animals called plankton (most of them are microscopic!). Plankton goes wherever the water takes it, and it's the beginning of most ocean food webs. It gets eaten by fish, whales, and other animals you'll meet on the next page. Check out the different kinds of plankton below!

Phytoplankton

Phytoplankton (FYE-toe-plank-tun) is a pretty big word for something so tiny! These microscopic floating plants use sunlight to make food and oxygen in a process called *photosynthesis*. This means that phytoplankton don't have to eat food—they just have to *be* food for other animals in the food web!

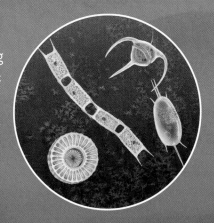

Zooplankton

As you might be able to tell from the word "zoo" in their name, zooplankton (ZOO-oh-plank-tun) are tiny animals. Many of them are baby fish, jellies, or crabs that are too small to see without a microscope. And what do they eat? Look out, phytoplankton!

Krill

These shrimp-like animals, about as long as your thumb, are a type of zooplankton. They eat other small zooplankton and phytoplankton. Millions and millions of krill may live together in a swarm large enough to show up in photos of Earth taken from space!

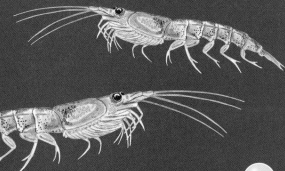

Plankton Eaters

Can you imagine eating rice one grain at a time? No way? Well, plankton eaters scoop up large amounts of plankton for the same reason—it's really hard to fill a stomach eating tiny things one by one. That's why many plankton eaters are "filter feeders," which means that they strain plankton out of the water to eat it.

Soft-Shell Clam

Soft-shell clams are filter feeders that suck water in through a tube called a *siphon*. As the water moves across the clam's gills, phytoplankton and tiny zooplankton in the water cling to the sticky mucous that coats the gills.

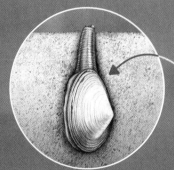

The soft-shell clam buries itself in the sand.

Moon Jelly

Jellies (commonly known as jellyfish) eat other plankton. Stinging tentacles catch plankton and pass it up the jelly's body to the mouth, located in the dome-shaped part, which is called the *bell*.

mackerel

Fish

Herring, mackerel, and other fish swim along, scooping up zooplankton as they go. As the seasons change, they travel to places where plankton are plentiful.

capelin

sand lance

herring

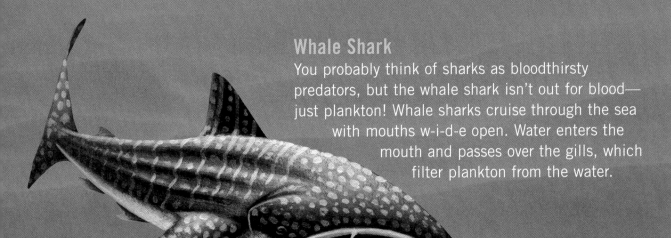

Whale Shark

You probably think of sharks as bloodthirsty predators, but the whale shark isn't out for blood—just plankton! Whale sharks cruise through the sea with mouths w-i-d-e open. Water enters the mouth and passes over the gills, which filter plankton from the water.

Baleen Whales

Blue whales, gray whales, and humpback whales are known as *baleen whales* because instead of teeth, they have plates made of baleen (material similar to your fingernails) in their mouths. They filter-feed by taking in a huge mouthful of water and pushing the water out through the baleen plates. Then they lick off the krill and other food left behind on the baleen like you would lick peanut butter from the roof of your mouth.

humpback whale

Turn the page to keep on climbing the food web!

Predators:
The Meat Eaters

Movin' on up in the food web, the predators rule. Instead of scooping and filtering like plankton eaters, meat eaters (called *carnivores*) do a whole lot more chasing, snatching, and nabbing. All that hunting means they catch their prey just one or a few at a time.

Leatherback Sea Turtle
These huge turtles slurp down slippery jellies with the help of spines in their throats.

Puffin
These seabirds rest on land only to nest and raise chicks. They spend most of their time swimming in the water and diving to catch food. Puffins snack on krill and also gobble up oodles of small fish, such as herring and capelin.

Harbor Seal
Seals eat fish, shrimp, and krill, and they usually swallow their prey whole. Squid and puffins also make tasty snacks for harbor seals!

Bottlenose Dolphin

The dolphin's sharp, cone-shaped teeth are perfect for snatching slippery fish (which the dolphin swallows whole). Sometimes dolphins hunt in groups and use their tails to stun fish, making them easier to catch.

Tiger Shark

There aren't too many animals a tiger shark won't go after. Fish, birds, sea turtles, horseshoe crabs, some whales, other sharks—and sometimes, people—are all on the menu.

Killer Whale

Killer whales do whatever it takes to catch a meal—chase prey, hunt together, herd fish into tight groups, tip over chunks of floating ice to get at seals and penguins, make big splashes to wash birds from rocks, and even deliberately lie on the beach to nab a sea lion snack. It's no surprise that these guys are at the top of the food web!

Get an inside look at the food web yourself—turn the page to see how you do at gulping down prey!

Gulp!

Okay, ocean explorer, you've read about ocean food webs, from plankton to sharks and all the animals in between. But do you really know your stuff? Try these two Gulp! card games to see if you've got what it takes to rise to the top of the food web!

What You Do
Part 1: Gulp War

If you've ever played the card game War, then you have a head start on the rules of Gulp War! Here's how to play:

1. Shuffle the cards so they're all mixed up.

2. Deal out the cards evenly, so you and your opponent each have half the cards. Keep the stacks face down.

3. Both players flip over the top cards of their stacks at the same time.

4. If the creature on your card eats the creature on your opponent's card, then take both cards and add them to the bottom of your stack. And of course, if your opponent's card gulps yours, you have to give it up!

5. If neither creature on the cards eats the other (or if you run into the one case where the two animals eat each other), it's a tie.

6. If there's a tie, each player flips over another card on top of the first one. Does one of those creatures eat the other? Keep flipping cards until one of the animals shown eats the other and the tie is broken. The player who plays the tie-breaking card gets all the cards that were laid down since the tie began!

7. The game continues until one player holds all the cards and is proclaimed "Top of the Food Web." Or, if you want to end the game earlier, set a time limit (like fifteen minutes). When the time's up, the player with the most cards wins!

the winner!

Check this list to see who eats who!

← tie →

← tie →

the winner takes all six cards!

Part 2: High-Speed Gulp

Now that you've got the hang of playing with your Gulp! cards, try this fast-paced game!

1. Shuffle the deck.

2. Lay two cards face down in the middle of the table. These will be the "gulp piles."

3. Deal the rest of the cards evenly into two face-down stacks—one for you, one for your opponent.

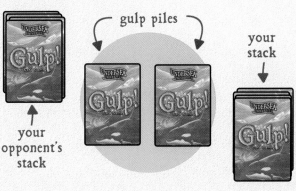

gulp piles

your stack

your opponent's stack

4. Each player takes the top five cards from his or her stack. Look at the five cards, but don't show your opponent.

5. On the count of three, each player flips over one of the cards in the middle.

6. Check the cards in your hand and see if you have a creature that eats or gets eaten by one of the creatures on the gulp piles in the middle of the table. If so, place your card on top of the correct gulp pile. You have to move fast, though, because if your opponent plays a card on that same gulp pile before you play *your* card, you lost your chance! You'll have to hang on to the card until you have another opportunity to play it.

7. Each time you put one of your cards onto a gulp pile, take another card from your stack so you always have five cards in your hand.

8. If no one has a card that will eat or be eaten by the gulp pile creatures, then each player takes the top card from his or her stack (or from the middle of a gulp pile, if there aren't any cards left on the stacks). On the count of three, each player flips his or her card onto one of the gulp piles.

9. The player who runs out of cards first wins the game!

Both players' cards can go on top of the squid—who will get there first?

PART 4:
Ocean Exploration:
The Last Frontier?

With undersea wonders like pearls, sunken treasure, and amazing plants and animals, it's no surprise that curious humans have been exploring the oceans for centuries. How deep can we go?

Deep!

Deep breath and down you go! From ancient times until just recently, that's all there was to ocean diving. Some divers used bricks and stones for extra weight to dive deeper.

Deeper!

But there's only so far you can go on one breath. To dive even deeper, you need some way to breathe underwater. Over the centuries, people came up with some pretty crazy ideas, such as trapping air in a barrel over their heads, or taking air-filled animal skins underwater.

Finally, in 1943, Jacques Cousteau and Émile Gagnan invented the Aqua-Lung. With tanks of compressed air and a device called a *regulator* to control the flow of air from the tanks, scuba (short for **S**elf-**C**ontained **U**nderwater **B**reathing **A**pparatus) diving was born. The ocean became the new frontier!

Deepest!

Scuba diving took divers to depths people had never been to before, but there's a limit to how deep people can go before the *water pressure* (the weight of the water above pressing down) becomes too much.

Submersibles—mini-submarines—were designed to handle the water pressure and help people explore the darkest depths. Check out the Sea Quest on the next page to find out how subs work!

Dive In!

Sea Quest

How does a submarine dive and rise? Believe it or not, it's a simple matter of plain old air and water! Make your own mini-sub to see exactly how it all works. Go ahead...*sink* into this Sea Quest!

What You Need

- Clear plastic soda bottle (1-liter or 2-liter)
- Mini-sub kit (pipette and bolt)
- Scissors
- Tall drinking glass
- Water

What You Do

1. Make sure the soda bottle is empty. (If it's not, you'll have to find a way to drink the rest in the name of science!) Then peel off the label and rinse out the bottle.

2. Push the bolt along the pipette, all the way to the bottom of the bulb.

3. Cut off the open end of the pipette about $\frac{1}{4}$ inch (.5 cm) from the bolt. This is your mini-sub!

4. Fill the drinking glass three-quarters full with water.

5. Grab the bulb of the pipette between your thumb and first finger and squeeze until your fingers meet in the middle. Dip the cut end of the pipette into the water and slowly move your finger and thumb apart to suck water into the pipette. The pipette should contain about one-third water and two-thirds air.

6. Drop the mini-sub, open end first, into the glass of water. If the sub floats with the bulb barely poking out of the water like Sub A, go on to Step 7. If the sub sinks like Sub B, or sticks way out of the water like Sub C, adjust the amount of water in the pipette until it floats like Sub A.

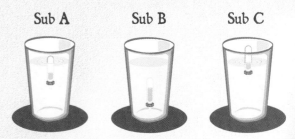

Sub A   Sub B   Sub C

If your sub's a sinker, take it out of the glass, squeeze a little water out of the pipette, and drop it back in the glass to see if it floats properly.

$\frac{2}{3}$ air

$\frac{1}{3}$ water

If your sub sticks out too far, take it out of the glass, squeeze *all* of the water out of the pipette, and repeat Step 5. This time squeeze the pipette even more to suck up more water than before.

7. Place the soda bottle in an empty sink or bathtub and fill the bottle with water to the very top.

8. Remove the sub from the glass. Don't squeeze any water out. Immediately drop the sub, open end first, into the bottle. A little water will overflow from the bottle—that's okay.

9. Screw on the bottle cap tightly.

10. Squeeze the bottle with both hands. *Zhoop*! There goes the sub down to the depths! When you stop squeezing, up it goes!

11. Squeeze the bottle a few more times. Do you notice how the water level in the pipette increases each time you squeeze, and goes back down when you let go? That's what makes the sub sink and rise!

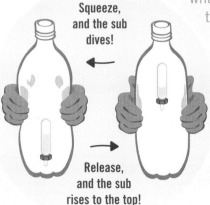

Squeeze, and the sub dives!

Release, and the sub rises to the top!

Sea the Point?

In this Sea Quest, you were working with a force called *buoyancy*—the force of water pushing up on something.

How does buoyancy work? Well, when you place an object in water, it pushes aside a certain amount of water. If the weight of that pushed-aside water is greater than the weight of the object, the object floats! Objects sink when they weigh more than the water they push aside.

At first, your sub floated because it contained lots of air (so it weighed less than the water it pushed aside). Then, when you squeezed the bottle, more water went into the sub (pushing the air into a smaller space). The added water made the sub heavier, so it sank.

When you released the bottle, the water level in the sub dropped, and the air took up more space again. The sub then became lighter and floated back up to the surface!

Real submarines dive and surface thanks to changing amounts of air and water, too. Check out the picture below to see how they work!

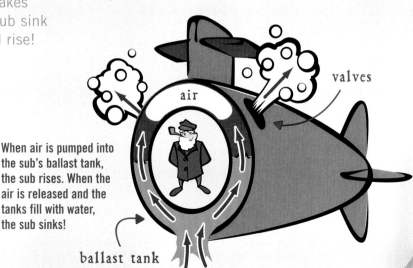

When air is pumped into the sub's ballast tank, the sub rises. When the air is released and the tanks fill with water, the sub sinks!

valves

air

ballast tank

seawater

Sinkable? — Unthinkable!

People thought the luxury liner *Titanic* was the best ocean liner ever built. They said, "She's unsinkable!" They couldn't have been more wrong. During her maiden voyage (that's sea talk for "first trip ever") from England to New York in 1912, *Titanic* hit an iceberg off the coast of Canada. More than 1,500 people died as the ship filled with water, broke in two, and plunged into the icy depths of the Atlantic Ocean— all in less than three hours. And there the ship stayed, undisturbed, for more than seventy years.

People were sure the *Titanic* was unsinkable.

Ocean Hide and Seek!

So, how do you find a shipwreck 2.4 miles (4 km) below the ocean's surface, where it's pitch black? In 1985, thanks to an undersea craft named *Argo* and technology called *sonar* (which you can learn about in the next Sea Quest), a team of French and American explorers were able to map the ocean floor near where the *Titanic* sank. After almost two months of searching, the team found the *Titanic*!

Argo, a remote-control submarine designed to work deep underwater, was the craft that discovered the *Titanic*. It wasn't until years later that submarines carrying people began to explore the wreck.

The front of the *Titanic*, called the bow, now sits on the ocean floor.

Sonar Challenge

How deep is the ocean? And what does the ocean floor look like? Scientists can answer these questions using a technology called *sonar* (short for **SO**und **NA**vigation **R**anging).

Sonar equipment sends down beeping sounds and then measures how long the sounds take to hit the ocean floor and bounce (or echo) back. We can create detailed maps of the ocean floor this way (and find shipwrecks, as you saw on the previous page)! Try this Sea Quest to see for yourself how sonar works!

What You Do
Part 1: Create an Ocean Floor!

First, you'll need an ocean floor to study—so have a friend make you one inside a shoe box!

1. Turn the box so it's lying on one of its long sides. Then, have an adult help you cut a slit down the middle of the top side. Make the slit as long as the box and as wide as the ruler.

cut slit to fit ruler

2. Go to another room while your friend creates an "ocean floor" in the shoe box by arranging objects of different heights in a row on the bottom. The objects should be taped down so they stay in place.

tape objects down

3. Once the ocean floor is finished, your friend should put the lid on the box and call you back to the room.

Part 2: Go for Sonar!

Now make a map of your ocean floor without ever laying eyes on it!

I. Lay the ruler lengthwise across the top of the shoe box, and make a mark with the pencil every inch (or centimeter) along the slit.

2. Make a chart like the one below to keep track of your depth measurements.

depth measurement chart
↓

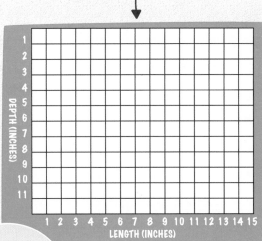

3. Drop the ruler in the slit at each of the inch-marks. How deep does the ruler go? Mark the depth for each inch on your graph.

4. Connect the dots you marked, then shade underneath the line to get a view of your ocean floor.

5. Open the box. Do the cliffs, plains, and trenches on your graph match the "real" ocean floor in the box?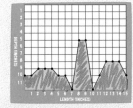

Sea the Point?

You measured the depth of your "ocean" by dropping in the ruler and measuring how far down it went.

Sonar works in a similar way, except sonar uses *sound* to measure the distance to the ocean floor. Sonar instruments send down "beeps" and measure how long the beeps take to bounce off the bottom and return to the surface. The longer it takes the beep to bounce back up, the deeper the spot!

You might have noticed that your graph didn't look *exactly* like your real ocean floor. That's because you only took measurements every inch—if you took more measurements, you'd have a better map.

Scientists make detailed maps of the ocean floor with a kind of sonar called multi-beam sonar. Instead of just measuring the depth of the water straight up and down in one spot, multi-beam sonar takes many measurements of an area at once. All these measurements can create a very accurate map of the ocean floor.

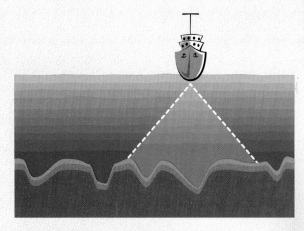

Multi-beam sonar can take sixty measurements from one place to give scientists detailed views of the seafloor.

SMALLEST OCEAN: Arctic Ocean

More than thirteen Arctic Oceans could fit into the Pacific Ocean! The Arctic Ocean is also the shallowest ocean—its average depth is only a quarter the depth of the Pacific.

WORLD'S LONGEST MOUNTAIN RANGE: Mid-Atlantic Ridge

If you put the Rockies, Andes, and Himalaya mountain ranges end to end, they would only stretch a quarter the length of the Mid-Atlantic Ridge. At 46,000 miles (74,030 km), this underwater mountain range just keeps going and going and going!

WORLD'S TALLEST MOUNTAIN: Mauna Kea, Hawaii

Though most people think Mount Everest is the tallest mountain in the world, it's only the tallest on *land*. If you measure from the ocean floor, Mauna Kea is the big one when it comes to mountains! It rises from the ocean floor and is about ¾ of a mile (1.2 km) taller than Mount Everest.

BIGGEST OCEAN: Pacific Ocean

The entire Pacific Ocean covers almost a third of the Earth's surface! The next biggest ocean, the Atlantic, is only half its size.

SALTIEST WATER: Weddell Sea, Southern Ocean

When sea ice forms, most of the salt is left behind in the surrounding water. In a single season, ice forms again and again in the Weddell Sea, which makes the water get saltier and saltier.

Ocean!

Your first course at Undersea U wouldn't be complete without a quick tour of the extremes of the ocean! Check out the map below to find out which ocean is the biggest...which is the saltiest...and, of course, where the deepest spot lies!

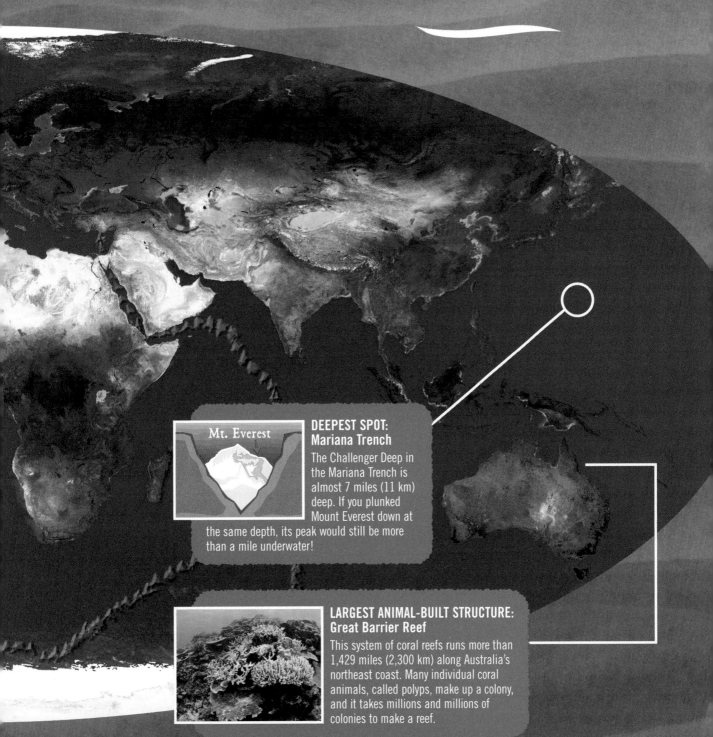

DEEPEST SPOT: Mariana Trench

Mt. Everest

The Challenger Deep in the Mariana Trench is almost 7 miles (11 km) deep. If you plunked Mount Everest down at the same depth, its peak would still be more than a mile underwater!

LARGEST ANIMAL-BUILT STRUCTURE: Great Barrier Reef

This system of coral reefs runs more than 1,429 miles (2,300 km) along Australia's northeast coast. Many individual coral animals, called polyps, make up a colony, and it takes millions and millions of colonies to make a reef.

Catch the Next Wave at UU!

Congratulations! You've arrived at the end of your first adventure at Undersea U! Are you dripping wet? Were all your Sea Quests a splashing success? And how are your pet triops doing?

You've soaked up a LOT of cool undersea info, like how currents and tides keep the ocean in motion, how marine animals feast under the sea, how subs sink and surface, and how sonar helps us map the ocean floor.

But that's only the tip of the iceberg! Undersea U will ship new books (and cool new undersea kits!) to you every month for the entire time you're on the Undersea U crew. Just check out the list below to see some of the topics that UU has in store for U!

So, keep an eye on your mailbox, because more undersea adventures are flowing your way!

Future UNDERSEA U Topics Include:

▶ The Fish Files   ▶ Sharks and Other Hunters of the Deep   ▶ Life in the Darkest Depths   ▶ Whales, Dolphins, and Other Marine Mammals

▶ Spineless and Squishy Ocean Creatures   ▶ Pirates   ▶ Shipwrecks and Other Disasters at Sea   ▶ The Future of the Ocean